Stopford Augustus Brooke

The ship of the soul

And other papers

Stopford Augustus Brooke

The ship of the soul
And other papers

ISBN/EAN: 9783741176388

Manufactured in Europe, USA, Canada, Australia, Japa

Cover: Foto ©Andreas Hilbeck / pixelio.de

Manufactured and distributed by brebook publishing software (www.brebook.com)

Stopford Augustus Brooke

The ship of the soul

SMALL BOOKS ON GREAT SUBJECTS.

Pott 8vo, in Buckram Cloth, price 1s. 6d. each.

1. **Words by the Wayside.** By GEORGE MATHESON, M.A., D.D., F.R.S.E., Minister of the Parish of St. Bernard's, Edinburgh. [Second Edition.
2. **Faith the beginning, Self-surrender the fulfilment, of the Spiritual Life.** By JAMES MARTINEAU, D.D., D.C.L., Author of "Endeavours after a Christian Life," "Hours of Thought," &c. [Second Edition.
3. **Reconsiderations and Reinforcements.** By J. M. WHITON, Ph.D., Author of "Beyond the Shadow," &c.
4. **Mischievous Goodness,** AND OTHER PAPERS. By CHARLES A. BERRY, D.D.
5. **The Jealousy of God,** AND OTHER PAPERS. By JOHN PULSFORD, D.D., Author of "Quiet Hours," &c.
6. **How to Become like Christ,** AND OTHER PAPERS. By MARCUS DODS, D.D. [Second Edition.
7. **Character through Inspiration,** AND OTHER PAPERS. By T. T. MUNGER, D.D., Author of "The Freedom of Faith," "The Appeal to Life," &c.
8. **Chapters in the Christian Life.** By the Ven. W. M. SINCLAIR, D.D., Archdeacon of London.
9. **The Angels of God,** AND OTHER PAPERS. By JOHN HUNTER, D.D.
10. **The Conquered World,** AND OTHER PAPERS. By R. F. HORTON, M.A., D.D.
11. **The Making of an Apostle.** By R. J. CAMPBELL, of Brighton.
12. **The Ship of the Soul,** AND OTHER PAPERS. By STOPFORD A. BROOKE, M.A.

Small Books on Great Subjects.—XII.

THE SHIP OF THE SOUL.
    By STOPFORD A. BROOKE, M.A.

THE SHIP OF THE SOUL,
And Other Papers.

By Stopford A. Brooke, M.A.

LONDON: JAMES CLARKE & CO.,
13 & 14, Fleet Street.   1898.

First Edition, November, 1898.

Contents.

	PAGE
The Ship of the Soul	1
The Triumph over Life	16
The Christian in the World	31
The Risen Life	47
The Calming of the Storm	60
God's Education of Man	82
Faithfulness until Death	95

The Ship of the Soul.

"Be sober, be vigilant."

WE are this first day of the year like a fleet of ships about to set sail on a new voyage. As yet we lie in harbour, making ready for the ocean-way, and a motley group we are. Some are great ships, some small; some are newly launched, and some have borne for many years the winds and dangers of the deep seas of life. Some know the great water-paths, and others have no experience. But one and all seek happiness; though what the happiness is, and of what kind, varies as varies the character and the past of the captain of each ship. Each has the Happy Isles before him, and the aim to reach their shore. It is an undying hope; and those who have most often made in vain the voyage are as eager in their hearts—nay, it may be, more eager than those who set sail for the first time—to seek their paradise. For, save in those who refuse, through inglorious ease, to strive any more with danger and towards unknown lands, the ideal does not die. No age can wither the love of the perfect, no experience of failure dash its effort; it looks upward with a youthful face, even in the arms of death.

And to-day we begin. The sails are spread; the wind blows freshly from the land; we lift the anchor, and one by one round the pier, and before us is the wide and tumbling sea. And from silent witnesses, encompassing us like a cloud, great cheer arises, wishing us good fortune; but good fortune won by heroic endurance, heroic act, and by an heroic heart; wishing us the strength of God our

Father, and the grace of our Lord Jesus Christ; but the strength made ours by faith and prayer and watchfulness; by noble resistance to the storms of evil and the craft of sloth; and the grace made ours by love and hope and joy, that have their source in the life that Jesus led, and the doctrine that He taught. "Farewell!" they cry. "Live well, fight well, steer straight, keep a sharp look out, defend the right, succour the disabled ships, and find the islands of the blest who see God." With that cry in our ears we enter the open sea. How many of us shall return? Some will sink in mid-ocean, and perchance find underneath its waves the Happy Land. Others the storm shall smite, and they will return with shattered bulwark and riven sail to refit for the year to come. Others will bring back a noble cargo, or the news of some great discovery. Others will lose their way, and drift from one tract to another of forgotten seas, and we shall not meet them again; and some will reach in peace, worn out with long sailing, the shores of heaven, the haven where they would be. We shall be sorrowful to miss their barks, but they will be glad at heart. And now, whom have we on board who may help and guard us in the dangers of the year? What qualities have we in the ship of the soul?

The first we need is Prudence. When Jesus said to us, "Take no thought for the morrow," He did not mean (as many of His parables make plain) that we should make no provision, through prevision, for the future. What He did mean was that we were not to spend our time in anxiety about the future, in worrying over matters which we could not help; but have that trust in God which enables us to act with freedom from over-cares. The prudence He counselled was the fortification of the soul against known dangers, and the building of character against unknown. By this time most of us know where we are weak, can tell fairly well what kind of troubles and temptations we shall meet. Do not start on your voyage without preparation against these. The worst are those dangers which we like, those temptations and sins we love. Against these—against drifting into them—we often make no provision, because we do not wish really to avoid them. Gather then yourselves together, strengthen your hearts, remember your high vocation, pray to the Lord for moral strength, foresee what is coming, and be ready to master your ship when the fatal current begins to drift you away. Take oil in your vessels with your lamps — to express it in the words of Christ. Before the temptation comes, strengthen the feeble parts of your defence, even though all your wishes be against it.

But the prudence which Christ advised was not only this which provides for the future. His method of defence lay much deeper. This, of which I have spoken, guards against known danger and trouble. But life is as full of surprises as the sea. In a moment, out of a clear sky, the lightning comes. In an instant, before we know what has happened, a new passion may leap upon us; or a new ocean in our hearts, of which we were unaware, opens before us, and all its waves cry, "Come and sail on our sunny surface"; and that of which we thought ourselves wholly incapable, which never occurred to us as possible, is suddenly done by us, suddenly known by us. We are like men who think they are in a dream, and who find out that it is no dream at all. This surprise within may be a good thing;

it may be an evil thing; and if it should be evil, what is our guard against it, what is our Christian prudence?

The method of Christ went to the root of the matter. He could not secure us against these surprises; He would not have done so if He could, for they belong to the education, the development of the soul; and we must find out what is within us, what we are. But He did warn and prepare us. In many sayings He told us that we were to form a character; to fill the heart with God; to accustom the soul to think and to feel justly, courageously, hopefully, joyfully, trustfully, truthfully. Out of the heart are the issues of life. Make it strong and right, and then, whatever surprise may come, you will not be unprepared; but ready at every instant to meet the unforeseen with the qualities which will claim and secure its good, which will recover from the surprise of evil, see through its false beauty, reject its allurement, and anchor amid its drifting. The best prudence, the best preparation for the changes and chances of life is that which is in the power of you all—the hourly formation and strengthening of a character like that of Jesus. Weave your will, chiefly by renunciation of all in it which injures love, into the character of God. Then you may with humility begin your voyage in joy and end it in victory.

So far for Prudence. Connected with it is Watchfulness. Prudence prepares before we start, counts the cost, provides the stores. Watchfulness is the continuance of this temper in the voyage, from hour to hour; but applied more to the wants and circumstances of the moment than to prevision of evil. It is having the soul awake, with its eye on the object, its loins girt for instant action, capable of presence of mind, and coolness of thought, and rapidity of plan, and swiftness of execution. And, indeed, we want that temper in life, for to be without it is not only to fail in the surprises of life—of these I have spoken, but to miss that of which I have not spoken—the opportunities in life which God gives us. Often, in the midst of sorrow, that event occurs which, if we could seize it, would enable us to spring off the evil shadow of sorrow and to keep only its beauty. And our eyes are blind. The happy thing we might have had passes us by within reach of our grasp, and offers us its hand, and sighs, and passes on. Often, in the midst of overwhelming trial, the crisis of the battle comes, and with the crisis the possibility of the action which will save us; and we miss the moment. We have allowed ourselves to be so confused that we cannot understand what we have to do, though it is often thundered in our ears. The hour fleets on, the occasion is lost, and we are beaten in the battle.

Again, we are sometimes only watchful towards arriving at the goal, and have neglected the need of watching all that is now around us. Our eyes are only fixed on the end —on the prize of peace—as if God were alone there, and not also on the wayside and in the common life through which we pass. And the goal is so far away that it brings tears into our eyes to think of it, and despair into our hearts, or it is so bright that it dazzles our sight. Then we weary, and sit down to weep; lost or spoilt by over haste. We should have watched the wayside also. God has provided for our journey a thousand beautiful things in nature which would cheer and exalt our spirits if we would love their beauty but a little. God has made everyday humanity, the common duties, the common affections,

so fair, so full of tenderness, so
full of claims on our love and
admiration, that, were we to watch
for them, and take their joy, the
path would be filled with music
and our souls with grace. It would
be lightened as a dusty road is
lightened by the murmur and the
song of a streamlet in the valley.
But we are so hurried that we
neither see nor hear, and the
beauty of life is lost, and its charm
unknown.

Others sail (for I return to my
lost comparison) and spend all
their days in the cabin where
their companions, the gods of this
world, sit and make their own bar-
barian merriment. These are the
great Cares with their worn faces,
who wear out the lives of men,
and yet are loved liked women.
There sits the Deceitfulness of
Riches, swollen and blind. There
is the sea goddess, Pleasure, changing and reckless and devouring as
the waves. There is False Honour

with a scabbard and no sword. There is the Love of the Moment with her flattering eyes. There is Ambition, his golden robe wrapped round the fire that burns his heart. There is the Pride of Life, the painted harlot, wrinkled to the eyes. There all the well-dressed conventions, all the maxims in society; moving things that seem men and women, but full of machinery alone inside. And with these, how many of you will drink and eat and play and sleep all your voyage through?

That is not watchfulness. Watchfulness is to live on the deck in the open air, seeing that the work of the ship is done, and the course straight for God; but never so straight as not to turn aside, though it seem loss, to help another ship. It is not loss. For in such help, though it delay us days and seem to make us wander from the way, there is the greatest progress to the goal.

Yes, to live in the fresh air of simple day and night, abiding not with the perishing gods of the world, but with One eternal and invisible, though always near; apart from all the idols whose worship degrades; living for whatever things are true and just, and of the divine harmony, and of good report among men, and of the character of Jesus; having in hand all your crew— every faculty ready at the moment, and to awake to do the nearest duty in the most needful work— *that* is watchfulness; *that* be your sailing companion through the year.

But it is more than that. It is to look upwards, and daily call for inspiration, in faith that it will come. It is in the silence of the night to see the ever-burning stars of life, the ideas that God has given men to guide them on their way, and seeing them, to sacrifice self and all outward things to glorify them before men, to make men love them better than life itself. It is, as each sun rises o'er the wandering sea, to expect new revelations of the truth of God, and be ready to hail them, and take them, when they come, into your heart with joy. And it is, *when* you have done all this which belongs to the actual voyage of this life and to the ships that sail with you—and till you have done *that*, you have no right to contemplation—to stand on the prow, in the hours when you are alone, and the material world fades around you into mist, and look forth, in faith and hope and joy and prophetic love, for the undiscovered land where there shall be no more sea save the righteousness of God like the great deep. This is the Christian watchfulness. God grant it may be ours. These are the ship companions St. Paul presents to you for the coming year—sober prevision, keen-eyed vigilance, the first to use while you are starting on your voyage, the second to be your daily mate while you sail. They, unlike too many comrades on this earth, unlike too many denizens of the soul, will not betray you. You will not regret that you have loved them, for they bring with them the faithfulness of God. Take them, and keep them and love them. Use them in the love of the Father, and in the grace of Jesus Christ. And may the Lord bless you, and keep you, and cause His face to shine upon you, and give you peace, now and for evermore. Amen.

The Triumph Over Life.

"Bless the Lord, O my soul; and all that is within me, bless His holy name.
"Bless the Lord, O my soul, and forget not all His benefits;
"Who forgiveth all thine iniquities; who healeth all thy diseases;
"Who redeemeth thy life from destruction; who crowneth thee with loving-kindness and tender mercies;
"Who satisfieth thy mouth with good things; so that thy youth is renewed like the eagle's."

PSALM CIII. 1—5.

WHEN the writer of this psalm looked back on life, what did he see? He saw his iniquities, for he had done much wrong; he saw the diseases of body and mind by which he had been troubled; he saw that his life, moral, spiritual and perhaps physical, had been on the verge of destruction; he saw that the years as they had gone by had robbed him of his youth, of the power to see and soar like the eagle. But as he looked deeper he saw also that all which was corrupting and terrible in these things had passed away.

Yet, he was not young. He who talks of his youth being renewed has left youth far behind. He writes like a man who had had his experience, and whose experience had been severe. But, wonderful to say, the experience had not made him sad. He had fought through its woes and passed triumphant into sunlight on the other side. The Lord his God had been with him through his life—*that* was his conviction. And he knew that his sins had been forgiven, because he had gained the power of their opponent virtues —the only fact which does, or ought to, convince us of forgiveness. He felt that the diseases of his soul had left their weakness, but that they were healed, and that he would not need to go through them again. The moral diseases which easily beset us must often be exhausted before we can gain true health. The one thing is to be healed of them, and, accepting their results, to never have them again. With God by our side, sometimes consciously, sometimes unconsciously —that happy end is reached.

Again, the writer felt as we often feel, that he had emerged from the very gulf of destruction; that he had been, as it were against his will, rescued from moral suicide; that all his life had been redeemed by God. Therefore he burst out into joy and thanksgiving! He who had been through grave sorrows; who had known sin, disease, even destruction; who might have cursed life and shrieked at what men call Fate; cries out in unfeigned and unmistakable rapture—it is a very outburst of song—"Bless the Lord, O my soul; and all that is within me, bless His holy name. Bless the Lord, O my soul, and forget not all His benefits."

And in realising this joyful victory of the moral and spiritual powers; in the resurrection of his spiritual being into strength; in the leaving behind him in its own grave all that was dead in his past; in the great cry of his heart as he looked back — "I am not there, I am risen;"—his youth was renewed like the eagle's! It was a great triumph; for his best life came back in a higher and a stronger way, with now but little chance of failure. He could again, like the eagle, look upon the sun, and love the upper ranges of the sky; again soar but with steadier beat of wing than in youth; again possess the freedom he loved before disease and destruction had enslaved his plumes; again breathe the breath of immortal love; again in conscious union with God hear the great spheres " in measured motion draw after the heavenly tune." And certainty was now with this victory, for he had known and found the Father of his spirit. The waters of his new life arose out of the fountain Life of God Himself, and he knew from whence they came. There was now a source and goal for his ideals, hopes, efforts, for beauty he loved, and for universal joy. It was the Almighty Love and Life of loveliness Himself who was now in him—a personal friend, redeemer, strengthener, exalter; who crowned him with loving-kindness and tender mercies. This is the true resurrection; this is the triumph of life. This is the landscape on which we shall look at last from the peak of our attainment; for God is sworn to Himself to make it true for every human soul. It will not be for us alone; it cannot be otherwise than universal. Were it not so to be, Love would cease to be.

This, then, is a noble temper in

which to survey the past. And were that joy more common here, the world would be very different. The one sorrow is, that it takes so long to bring us to this point; that many never reach it on this earth. Well, we are here for so short a time; it is such a small portion of the road of our life that we travel; one stage alone in the vast years that belong to us—that we must not ask too much, but be content and bless the Lord. If, when we come to die, we have wrought out of our nature, hand in hand with our Father, one evil twist, one false form of passion; redeemed a few failures, made one crooked place straight for ourselves, or straight for others; we may think ourselves fortunate in life. Indeed, to smooth the path for others is the great need for our own nearness to God. It is in making the rough places gentle for our fellow-men, because we love them; in saving them from sin, false passion, or false aims in healing; their diseases; in redeeming their life from destruction, that we most certainly attain these blessings for ourselves; most surely become aware that God is with us; most gladly come to cry out at the end, "My youth is renewed like the eagle's; bless the Lord, O my soul, and all that is within me, bless His holy name!"

There is always the possibility of such a resurrection if we have retained certain things in life, which are, so to speak, the conditions on which God is known by us to be our own. They are Faith and Hope and Love, the virtues of the ideal world. I do not mean that these, in order to form this conditional state, should be directly felt towards God; or that they should exist in any high development; but they should at least be in germ within us, towards God, and displayed in action, towards men. When they are not cast aside or lost, God can be felt by us as acting in our soul; and so strange, so unexpected are the things that occur, that when we are suddenly touched by them, as it were from without, we cannot help feeling and saying to ourselves, "There is some One whom I know not at work on me, some One who cares for me, some One who has watched and laid His hand upon my life at the right moment; who now, just when all seemed broken to pieces, has opened to me a new garden of work and happiness, who bids me walk in it, forget my past, and renew my youth."

I could tell many stories of this happening to men who, like the writer of the psalm, had reached the middle term of life. I remember one who had been for a long time drifting towards an evil act which was certain to do more harm to others than to himself, but who had not as yet determined on flinging friends, society, work, good repute, his past and future, and God Himself, to the winds. The one thing that kept him back was a remnant of belief in God, in One beyond humanity, beyond the world's laws of convention and morality. Nothing else was left, for he had, in the desire for this wrong thing, passed beyond caring whether the whole world went against him, whether he injured others or no. He was as ready to destroy all the use of his own life as he was careless of the use of the lives of others. But he felt a slow and steady pull against him. He said to himself, "This is God, though I know Him not." At last, however, he determined to have his way. One day, the loneliness and longing had been too great to be borne, and when night came he went down his garden resolved on the evil thing. "This night," he said, "I will take the plunge." But as he went he heard the distant barking of a dog in the village; the moon rose above a dark yew tree at the end of the garden, and he was abruptly stopped in the midst of the pathway. Something seemed to touch him as with a finger, and to push him back. It was not till afterwards that he analysed the feeling, and knew that the rising of the moon over the yew tree and the barking of the dog in the distance had brought back to him an hour in his childhood, when in the dusk he had sat with his mother, after his father's death, in the same garden; and had heard her say—" When thou passest through the waters, I will be with thee, and through the floods they shall not overwhelm thee." It was this slight touch that saved him from wrong which would have broken more lives than his own. It was God speaking; but it would have been as nothing to him, had he not kept his little grain of faith in God alive, the dim consciousness that there was One who cared for him, who had interest that he should conquer righteousness. Next day, he left his home, travelled and won his battle; and his action redeemed not only his own, but another's life.

Take another story, of a man who had given up his whole life to love. At last, after many years, he felt that love was being given to him no more; and I shall not easily forget the words in which he described, with terrible force and brevity, the life of the two years he passed while he knew that all he cared for was gliding away from him, and in a way so unspeakably commonplace that it doubled his pain. It was the strangest thing that when the last stroke was given, when he received the letter which told him that his whole life for more than ten years was absolutely blotted out, irrevocably blackened, that he should have had laid before him, as if by a miracle, a wholly new life into which and its interests he was slowly drawn, so that healing came and light arose.

And when I asked him how it was that he could with any freshness, after such long torment, take up a new life, he said, "It was because I never lost love; whatever happened to me I went on loving; whatever commonplace came round me I always clung to the ideal; whatever change came in others I was always constant to love. When the crash threw down my palace, though I was miserable, I was not embittered; though I was stripped of everything, my soul was still young; love had kept the springs of life flowing in my heart. There was never a desert in my soul. Therefore, though I never loved again, I was able to live a fresh life; and on the very day when I knew the old was entirely hopeless, I looked round and felt that God had opened a new world before my eyes. But I never should have known that a new life was possible had I not kept within my soul love—pure, constant, ideal, and fresh—and let nothing embitter it.

These stories illustrate the psalm; they illustrate the temper of the soul which makes resurrection possible, even in later life; which receives the word of God, and brings forth fruit, some thirty, some sixty, and some a hundredfold. Faith in One who, far beyond the custom of the world, has personally to do with us; whose interest in us is supreme; who, touching us always, touches us specially when we need it; who is sworn to lead us till we can say with Jesus, I and my Father are one—this is the victorious principle of life. And Love, never allowed to fall into scorn, kept ideal, kept untouched by the world—that keeps in us the capacity for new life, the power of hearing the voice of Jesus, the power of receiving into a contrite heart the love of God the Father.

Afterwards, these things become more and more divine, more and more religious. He that is faithful in the least, will be faithful also in the greater. He that is faithful in human things, will also be faithful in divine things. He who loves man faithfully will come in the end to love God faithfully. And God will fill with His own love the soul which has been abandoned by earthly affection. The heart that trusts in Him and loves Him, will not be sent empty away. And it is better that God should so fill us, after we have gone through our trouble; for His love never disappoints, suffers no caprice, is touched by no betrayal, does not diminish but increase in good and power and joy—till the whole heart, catching fire from God, renews its youth like the eagle. We shall be thrilled with higher joy, keener excitement than we felt when we were young, before the days of pain; we shall see the perfect fulfilment of our ideal, and looking back upon our past, cry with the Psalmist:—

Bless the Lord, O my soul; and all that is within me, bless His holy name.
Who satisfieth thy mouth with good things; so that thy youth is renewed like the eagle's.

The Christian in the World.

"I pray not that Thou shouldest take them out of the world, but that Thou shouldest keep them from the evil."—JOHN XVII. 15.

THE last words of Christ to his disciples, clustered round him in that solemn hour when he took leave of them before he died, were prayer. It was a prayer as reported to us, which threw into pregnant words the meaning of his whole work, but it was also steeped in the tender thought which fills the heart of one who parts from those he has long loved. As he prayed for those around him, who were to spread among men the good news of God, commending them to his Father's care, every word is touched with the human tenderness of separation. "Holy

Father, keep through Thine own name those whom Thou hast given me, that they may be one"—one in love, one in that Will of God which is the bond of love. "Keep them from the world, not from the outward world, but from the evil of the world." With that prayer Christ defines the position of his followers in their life among men, and the meaning of it is our subject.

What is Christ's meaning for the term "world"? It is this passing scene of time, with its transient pleasures and sorrows, pursuits and loves; and the mass of men that live for these alone. There is the world of men, of business, of politics, of labour for wealth and fame—the storm of life in which we sail. "Pray," men say, "to be taken out of that; out into the deserts or the quietude of our retired rooms; in solitary meditation to live the life of God." "I do *not* pray," said Christ, "that you should be removed from that—only from its evil."

The spirit of this prayer was the practice of his life. His was not the fanaticism of the ascetic, or the devout dreaming of the convent; his was the life which moved in cities, and collected around it the countryman, the fisherman, the labourer, the publican, the sick, the hungry, all shades and classes of mankind; in active giving and receiving, in vivid sympathy with the domestic, social, and universal life of men. And that is our life, we who desire to follow Christ; he will be nearest to us, and God will be most with us, when we are doing our daily work most vigorously in the midst of the world.

When we see our calling as the will of God for us, as the place He has set for us to keep, and in which we are to reveal His will and promote His work—then, out of this worldly calling, good and power will daily flow into our character, and all its evil will be kept far away. Pray every morning, not that you may be taken out of this world of work, but that you may be guarded from its sin.

There are worlds in which we move, other than the world of business. There is the passing world of human love. Decay besets it, passions injure it, life wears it out, sin corrupts it, death seems to shatter it into pieces. This is its passive evil, that it fleets away. But it has also active evils. The love of home is mixed with too eager a desire for wealth, with too absorbing an interest to push our way into society, because we want a good position for our children. We often sacrifice to home the great social interests of men, and establish selfishness within our family. Then, too, love may become so slavish through jealousy, so enthralling through sensual passion, as to rob us of the power of work, or of the vision of God. These are evils of the world of love, and Christ prays to God that we may be kept from them—but he does not pray that we may be kept out of the world of love.

Then there is also the world of youthful enjoyment, in which to live and breathe is happiness. There is the world in which we live with nature—an enchanting world indeed to those who care for it. And, as manhood deepens, two other worlds are ours, the world of art, where beauty seeks for ever its ideal form; and the world of knowledge, wrought by thought out of the long results of time, created by science out of the past and the present, out of the heaven above us and the earth beneath.

These, too, are of the things that pass away. Disease and death lay their hand on youthful strength and joy; our pleasure perishes, and as we grow older our beauty grows colder as death draws near; knowledge vanishes before an ever-increasing knowledge; even the love of nature departs at last when the senses lose their power, and only the memory of the loveliness we have seen endures. Death is merciless to them all.

Alas! they possess, not only the passive evil of fleetingness, but also active evils. Unchastened joy shuts out the vision of God, makes us forget the solemn work of life, bids our own wild will and not God's righteous will be master, and keeping us careless, frivolous and passionate, often ends in the bitterness of a wearied and unsatisfied old age. Unbridled love of nature separates us from man; so does unbalanced love of knowledge or of art. We should pray with Christ not to be taken out of these things, but to be kept from the evil that belongs to them. Even more we should pray to be kept from their spiritual evil. For love of nature, or love of art, being passions which derive their food from the senses, tend when men live in them, without one thought of God, to sensualise the conscience and the spirit; and the vast world of the invisible dies in us. This earth becomes all in all to us; decay becomes our chief fear, and death our worst evil. And it is just as possible to let the love of knowledge so master us that it usurps the whole of life. Then the spirit pines and dwindles for want of food; even more swiftly than in the absorbing love of beauty we lose the sight of God, forget the world from whence we came and whither we are going, and lose the powers of the soul.

Well, looking at all this, seeing clearly the evil of these passing worlds, men have said "that to abandon them is unworldliness, *is* the religious life; that to live without love, to shut the eyes to nature, to leave the business of men, to forswear art, to stifle knowledge, is to live for God." Christ does not say so. "I pray not that Thou shouldest take them out of the world, but that Thou shouldest keep them from the evil in it."

These worlds in which we live are, when separated from their active evils, beautiful, true, and needful; they ought to ennoble our hearts and bring forth good for men. By them, and through our life in them, the great being of mankind is civilised, educated, wrought towards perfection. To neglect them is to neglect our duty to mankind. Through true life in them our personal character, also, is built up. They are not our life, it is true, but through them God trains our life. And it is the very element of fleetingness in them which makes them into education. They die, but their results remain, built up into the soul.

We may be left at last without love, homeless and alone; but the gentleness, the forbearance, the long habit of loving observance of others, the rooted self-forgetfulness that has grown into a great tree within us; the faith in the beauty of human nature; the love which learnt at last to give up all for others—these things, born out of our life with nature and man, with knowledge and love and beauty,—live, and God exalts them into spiritual powers. We may be left, at last, it is true, unable to see the landscape, unable to thrill with joy, unable to shape into beauty that which we have seen and felt; but, when these powers have fled away, we cannot take out of your heart the power of delight that we have won, the refinement we have gained, the delicacy and purity of thought that these things have established in us, the inner music of truth and life which these, while they lasted, gave to our soul. God takes these powers of imaginative life, and makes them foundations of spiritual powers which aspire to find in Him the fountain of Joy, the source of Beauty, the everlasting light of Life and Truth. We may be left at last, conscious that we know nothing, that knowledge has fled away from us; but the power of concentration of intellect and of will that we have gained while we wrought in the world of knowledge; the strength and resolve that we have implanted in our will by mastering the difficulties that lay before us; the increased desire to push forward and never to be content with knowing—these, rooted in the character, God takes, and, fitting them to eternal objects, makes them, not only into powers of the brain, but into powers of the soul. Yes, it was divinely wise of Christ to say, "I pray not that they be taken out of the world."

So far for the larger view of the matter. The more personal view remains, and I will make it personal to that in our life which most leads us to desire to leave the world. The world in which the Apostles were about to live was a world of trouble. It was Christ's own prophecy: "In the world ye shall have tribulation." It was a natural thought then to some of them that, looking forward to so serious and so sad a life, they should wish to pass at once by death to the glory their Lord had promised them; and still more natural that when they were afterwards involved in trial, they should say to their Father, "Take us from the world to Thyself; in rest give us Thy perfection."

It is the wish and thought of many now. Some are so tired with pain and trouble; others so harassed with themselves; others in so impossible a set of circumstances; others caught in so swift a backwater, out of which for all their passionate anger they cannot get; others so profoundly angry with life because they cannot have what they want—that one and all desire to have done with the whole of the scene of life; tortured with its tragedy, weary of its comedy, sick of its farce. It is very natural, and there are some who think it very spiritual. It is not spiritual, but selfish and faithless; it is not honourable, but cowardly. It is the part of a deserter to run away from life, even to desire to run away from it.

We are like soldiers given a post to keep, who know not how much depends upon their fidelity. We are placed here to face death if it should come, but not, because we are tired, to seek it, and rob the army of mankind of our work and vigilance. It is as dishonourable to seek for death because we are troubled with or afraid of life, as it is to run away from a battle because we are afraid of dying. We are born not only to be happy, but to endure hardness, as good soldiers of Jesus Christ. Our endurance saves and strengthens others of whom we know not, and knits our own character into the power and worth of a veteran of the cross. To be fit to live is to be fit to die. Until we can learn to live bravely, we cannot die bravely.

We are placed here to be trained for another and higher life. A certain time and certain trials upon this earth are necessary to develop us into the likeness of God's character. The aloe takes a hundred years to make a flower, the primrose a few spring days; some trees reach maturity in half a century, others weave their strength of folded fibres out of the rain, and wind, and sunshine of a thousand years. Each has its own period. It is so, also, with us, the planting of the Lord. A few trials, a few years, and some of us flower into all the perfection we can attain on earth. Many long years, bitter and protracted trials are the lot of others, before a single blossom can spring upon their lives; but—and it is a law which ought to console us—in proportion to the length of time and the greatness of the trial, is the fitness of the character for work, and the greatness also of the work that it has to do. The primrose is beautiful and cheers the heart of the passing traveller, and rejoices the Maying children who weave it in a wreath for their queen—and that is useful and lovely work, and has its place. But the oak shelters a thousand herds, and plants a forest; and builds the bulwark of the coast, and the fleets that unite the nations. We have no right to be impatient if God is making us into the heart of oak, which will, when the woodman death has felled us, give shelter and bring blessing to thousands in the other world. Not an hour of the time, not a single agony of the trial is lost; everything that we suffer here is transmuted otherwhere into strength and usefulness, into greatness and beauty of character.

Therefore, finally, do not pray to be freed from a world of trial; but pray to have the temper which will prevent suffering and trial becoming, through impatience or petulance, cowardliness or weakness of will, evil and not good to you. God placed His purest Son in the forefront of the battle, not that he might fall, but that he might conquer; not that he might die, but that he might live and contend for men. That is our noble calling, and well did Christ know how to kindle and inspire the human heart, when he told us that he needed us to live that we might save, ennoble, and comfort men; and in that work become at one with him, and at one with God. "I pray not that Thou shouldest take them out of the world, but that Thou shouldest keep them from the evil."

The Risen Life.

"If ye then be risen with Christ, seek those things which are above, where Christ sitteth on the right hand of God.

"Set your affection on things above, not on things on the earth.

"For ye are dead, and your life is hid with Christ in God." COLOSSIANS III. 1-3.

THIS is a description of the Resurrection life that the Christian should live in the present world. It is to be a life hidden with Christ in God. How can we live such a life, men and women ask, in the midst of the business and many cares of the world?

Some answer by retiring from the world, by isolating their manners, dress, or social habits from those of others, by forming themselves into a phalanx of opposition to the customs of society and its modes of thinking. This is not the Christian, but the Pharisaic life. Yet we must by no means think that all who hold that opinion, or who lead such a life outwardly, are Pharisees at heart. Many of them conscientiously believe it is the right way to live, and wear the dress of the Pharisee with the spirit of the Publican.

Nevertheless, the true Christian life wears the common dress of humanity. "It makes all things kin. It does not stand out angular against any part of mankind." Its mark is that humble spirit which is, in the sight of God, of great price. It does not dogmatise, it does not exclude. It is meek and lowly of heart; it has rest within itself, and brings rest to others. Its kingdom is not of this world, though its work is here, and therefore its servants do not fight. It does not strive, nor cry, nor is its voice heard in the streets. It is content to grow like the violet, hidden from the eye, known only by its scent; universal as the daisy, giving, like it, a "sympathy which cares not should it be set at naught;" shining in unexpected nooks among the rocks and fields of common life; in meekness, like that flower, fulfilling its "function apostolical." Read the Beatitudes, that is its charter. Read the chapter of St. Paul on charity—that is its spirit and its activity.

There is no work in the world which may not be wrought in the spirit of that chapter; yet we are told that the work of the world and the Christian life are incompatible. It is a great mistake. We have divided it too much from practical life, we have edged it round with rules and observances which isolate it from society; so that when men are asked to live the life of one who has risen with Christ, they answer "It is impossible." It is wise then to make what it is a little plainer, though not less difficult; a little simpler, though not more comfortable.

Take public life. This is the sphere in which a Christian life is most often declared to be impossible. But the Christian life is in the imitation of Christ for the love of his noble humanity, and that does not lead you away from the world; it only bids you rise above the spirit of the world. It is to have Christ's high standard of righteousness and love; and to live as close to it as we can, exerting all our strength. It forbids the tricks by which men enter Parliament; it forbids the corruption of others by any means whatever; it forbids the violation of conscience for the sake of party, or the sake of a seat. It forbids the business man to use the money of others in chance speculation; it bids him keep his hands clean, and his honour untainted, not only before the world, but before the tribunal of his own conscience. It tells him he has no right to go by the current standard of commercial morality—a standard which seems to say : "Get all the money you can by any means which will not bring you into the grasp of the law, or under public shame." It tells you to believe men, rather than to suspect them; to give a courteous honour to an adversary, rather than the dishonour of abuse; to have the justice which sees your own value and that of your opponent and allots the fitting meed to both. These, and many other things, are a part of the resurrection life of Jesus in public affairs.

Another side of public life is our life in society. The best way in which we may in heart and mind rise there with Christ, is by the thoughtful watchfulness of love. Thoughtlessness of heart slides into insensibility of heart, and, if encouraged in youth, makes the cruel men and women of after life. How often do we ask ourselves before we speak whether our speech will do wrong or give pain? We are proud sometimes of speaking daggers, and delight in the cleverness which makes another wince. It is a pride and pleasure which is base; for it is inhuman, and it is as far removed from the gentleness and sweetness of Christ as heaven is from hell. Then, again, there is that careless habit of "plain speaking," and the way we have of pluming ourselves upon it—till it passes with some into overbearingness, and with others into acute disagreeability. We little think how much it jars upon persons more sensitive than ourselves, and how much suffering it gives. It is good to be plain-spoken, but within the limits of charity. Still more mischievous is that looseness of tongue which proclaims everything that its owner has heard from another without a thought whether he may like what has been said in a moment of abandon to be proclaimed upon the housetops; which seems to think that nothing is sacred to feeling; and that no seal of confession, though not exacted, ought to be understood as laid upon the lips. That is abominable want of thought and love.

Worse still, as not only careless, but wicked, is the airy slander which gossips away a character in an afternoon, and runs lightly over a whole series of acquaintances, leaving a drop of poison on them all. The things thus said are said for ever. Years after the light word was spoken, we may find that it has made a whole life unhappy, or ruined the peace of a household. It was well said by St. James, "If any man among you seem to be religious and bridleth not his tongue, this man's religion is in vain." These are evil and vile things which arise from want of thought and watchfulness—watchfulness that can be only exercised and supported by the perseverance in us of the grace of Christ.

Much of what has been said about social life applies to domestic life. That which most spoils it, when love is there, is petty quarrels. I do not speak of differences of opinion upon subjects worthy of discussion. Abundance of discussion within the household keeps its atmosphere fresh; enlivens and stimulates the intellect, heart, and conscience of the family. I speak of quarrels. Familiarity of life with one another gives room for unchecked development of temperament; and when opposed temperaments do not care to play gently in and out among one another, ungracious disturbances ruffle the surface of our happy lake of life. Let them continue day by day, and these tempers, once so unfrequent, never let the waters rest. Love remains, but life is spoiled. Therefore, let the music of these words enter into your spirit, and keep them with you, till you learn how to make their meaning into daily act—" Learn of Me ; for I am meek and lowly of heart, and ye shall find rest to your souls."

One or two examples, out of many, may show how this gentleness of the Christian life may be attained. If you have been in the wrong from impetuosity or heat of temper, and for the moment been betrayed into sharp words or rude manners—then follow without false shame the guidance of your heart; say that you are sorry, not with the haughtiness which contradicts your words, but with the courtesy of love. To apologise for ill-doing or harsh speech is not ignoble. It is the offended isolation, it is the selfish sulkiness, which is unworthy of man or woman. The apology may be difficult at first, but difficulties of this kind we are bound to overcome if we seek to rise with Christ. At each successive time it becomes easier, and the doing of it prevents the recurrence of the temper which rendered the apology necessary. Again, if blame has to be given, wait till your personal irritation is over. It often comes in just as well, and more forcibly, a week or a month after, and when all your own anger is fled. But blame must sometimes be given directly. There are times when principle is involved, when one must speak at once to wife, or husband, or child, or friend. But be natural in it; let your heart speak and not your intellect alone: and, moreover, let all blame be rapid, and never repeat it. But, lastly, remember that in public, social, and domestic life, love is not, when unguarded, all in all. It must be accompanied by the right reason of justice; for justice is the only element in which love can act without the danger of falling into weakness, favouritism, or folly. Indeed, justice is the other side of the Shield of Love.

These little matters may seem slight, but in faithfulness of love among them, and in watchfulness of thought around them, the greater part of the resurrection life with Jesus lies hidden. When you have gained the spirit of his power in them, that spirit will expand to meet the demands of larger duties; and you will know that you are nearing day by day to that ideal life of yours, which, now hidden with Christ in God, is waiting for you in the ascended life of the future. It is consolation to think of it, when we have done our work. In the midst of this resurrection life (which, though risen out of sin and into victory, is yet sorely troubled) we are, in the quiet hours of sadness, permitted to look forward to the perfect life with God. As in the story of Jesus, so with us, the Ascension will be the sequel of the Resurrection.

Be not, then, too weary of your watchfulness; for this long struggle through public, social, private life, will not be for ever. "I go to my Father," said Jesus, "and I shall prepare a place for you." It is a happy thought. It speaks of peace to come, rest in a quiet country where our trouble shall be over, and yet our rest be not the rest of inactivity. It tells us of a life of perfect love, where all doing and thinking, being loved, are done and thought with pleasure; where jealousy shall not make affection torment; where concealed impatience of delaying friendship does not wear the mask of an indifference which wearies into pain the wearer's heart; where work will be no longer enervated by passion; where passion itself will replace feverish excitement by calm intensity; where, instead of wilfully giving pain because we love cruelly as the grave, we shall give pleasure because we know and trust. It is to this ascension life that our dying eyes shall look when the last hours are upon us. The vision is nearest then. We close our eyelids, and in a moment the world is gone. Death has touched us, and lo! the sunshine and the peace of Heaven! At last, we have ascended.

The Calming of the Storm.

"And when He was entered into a ship, His disciples followed Him. And, behold, there arose a great tempest in the sea, insomuch that the ship was covered with the waves; but He was asleep. And His disciples came to Him, and awoke Him, saying, Lord save us: we perish. And He saith unto them: Why are ye fearful, O ye of little faith? Then He arose and rebuked the winds and the sea; and there was a great calm. But the men marvelled, saying, What manner of man is this, that even the winds and the sea obey Him!"
MATT. VIII. 23-27.

On as wild a storm as this upon the Lake of Galilee, and at the time when the story rose into importance, the bark of the Church was tossed. Christianity, severed more completely than before the destruction of Jerusalem from its Jewish origins, had now become frankly Gentile, and the opposition of the Judaic communities deepened

THE CALMING OF THE STORM. 61

around it. Moreover, some years before this time at which I suppose the story took its final clothing, Nero had directed the painful attention of the Roman world to the Christian sect. It had been persecuted. Since then, its great expansion had made it a political element in the empire; and its direct attack on the worship of the Emperor made it dangerous to the Roman Peace in the towns. Therefore, on account, not of its religious, but of its political, results, it drew upon it now the iron hand of Rome.

From the Jews, then from Rome, the storm gathered round the ship; the waves threatened to overwhelm it; above the dark clouds the people of Christ could not see God; fear and depression fell upon them; their Master Jesus seemed asleep. "Lord, save us, we perish!" was their cry. But persecution taught its noble lesson. Their faith returned. Again they seemed to hear the words of Jesus: "Why are ye fearful, O´ ye of little faith?" Again the calm of courage and trust descended into their hearts. The storm passed by, and the Church had peace.

On as wild a storm are we ourselves often tossed in life. We reel to and fro on our ship, and stagger like a drunken man, and are at our wits' end. As manifold as our characters, so manifold are our tempests—tempests of sorrow; overwhelming storms of joy in which our wiser life is shipwrecked; hurricanes of passion, followed by weakness of will and fainting of conscience, so that if we have escaped the terrible wind, the summer breeze of trial that succeeds it is enough to break up our ship. Sometimes in the night of trouble fear besets us, and we lose the bearings of the lights of life, and rush blindly on the rocks. Sometimes the deeper darkness of conscious wrong settles down on life; we remember our innocence of old, we remember God whom once we loved, and, like Adam of old, we hide ourselves for shame from both remembrances. Then the wild wind and the darkness grow louder and gloomier. We lose our faith in God, and losing that, all our personal pain is more terrible. And sometimes then, apart from our own shame and wrong, we look forth on the ocean, and mark how hard and fierce is the storm on others, how heavily they labour in the waves, how many, crying out with shrieks that divide the night, go down in the black solitude, while God seems careless of their sorrow and their ruin!

"Where is He?" we ask, then, "who bore and conquered storms of old? Where is my Master Jesus, who used to wake and watch with men through life? Asleep? Where is He whose spirit will inspire me to find my Father again? Where is He whose faith will kindle mine till courage rise out of faith and peace out of courage? Still asleep? Save, Lord, I perish, I and all my fellows."

There is but one answer ever given by Him, and it has been always the same through the ages: "Why are ye fearful, O ye of little faith?" Belief in God, in a Father's love, in His care for you, in His care for all—that is the victorious power in the storms of life. It was at the root of the immortal peace of Jesus. It was at the root of the peace that possessed the spirit of the Church in the days of persecution. It is at the root of our peace. When we gain it there is a great calm, and there is nothing else which will bring us calm.

This is one of the great declarations of Christ's religion, and not only of His religion, but of all the great religions. But it is an answer which many cannot accept, which many will not accept. It conflicts often with the understanding; and there are thousands who think that the understanding is the best guide of life. It makes a demand on human pride which pride resents. Moreover, experience, till faith is felt, seems often against it; and what we see appears often to be the whole truth—that vain and common error. In all these cases we think there are other ways of getting through the storm. It is not through faith in a Father that we think we shall arrive at peace. There are other ways, we imagine, and some of these I speak of now.

We may have been so beaten by the tempest that we have given up all faith in God. Then we are often thrown wholly on ourselves, and we think our own will sufficient for the day. "My help," we say, "is in myself and time. I cannot get rid of this trouble, but if I wait, it will die away. The tempest will blow itself out. All I have to do is to keep fast hold of the rudder, and trim what sails are left, and not let courage go; ready for the sunlight, should it break through the clouds, ready for destruction should it come, and resolved at least to be undismayed."

And many work in that fashion through the wilder hours of life, and pass into quiet, not much damaged at first; and then, refitting their bark, set sail again. But the misfortune of that way is that the solitary self-confidence of their character, which up to a certain point is good, is developed beyond that point, and becomes self-pride. And self-pride (which, indeed, a thousand experiences has proved to be the worst of the things which ruin men and great causes) is that very quality which trust in some one, such as a Divine Father higher than ourselves, would make impossible. Faith in God prevents the destruction which follows pride in one's self. And that destruction comes in this way. After a time these solitary, self-sufficing persons become sick of themselves. Self has that wearying power. It feeds on its own heart. It sees itself and nothing else, everywhere, and that is a dreadful sight ; so dreadful that finally, the loathing of its company weakens the whole nature of its victim. It weakens even self-confidence in the end; and that quality, (which in conjunction with trust in God is good), now becomes mere rigidity of temper, loses its elasticity, and when the next storm comes, breaks like a steel rod, brittle from too great rigidity. This has been the fate of many; and what they reach in the end is not peace, but hardened hatred of life.

If the storm—to take a particular example — has been one of sorrow, and is met in this lonely, self-sufficing way, without any trust in the love of God—the most beautiful and certain result of which is a deep-seated tenderness for all mankind—the man, when he has emerged from the tempest, is harder, less kindly, less gentle than before. He has been so hard with himself that he thinks he is licensed to be hard with others; and he is harder because he does not care now so much as before for trouble. He is, in himself, less sensitive to pain. He has beaten sorrow and suffering, and he demands that others should beat it in the same way. But he asks too much of men, and he asks it too severely; and the result is that he is severed from mankind. He can give them no more help in trouble. This result proves that his way of conquering is wrong. He has missed all the uses of trouble. It ought to have made him softer-hearted, more gentle to failings, more sensitive, less selfish, less austere, less rough. It has made him the opposite to these graces of character.

Then, again, suppose that the storm has been caused by wrong-doing. Then, if we fight through the gale of punishment in this haughty fashion, we come out of it without any true repentance. The storm has been only a weariness, a disagreeable consequence, and no more. It has told us nothing which makes us hate the sin which caused it; nothing which will give us a motive to avoid it in the future—if it be agreeable. We have no sense of having been unworthy children of a Father who is righteousness and desires our righteousness; that mighty motive against sin which faith in God creates.

And the result is that we are often confirmed in the doing of our own will, even when we know that our will desires wrong. The storm of natural punishment blows itself out, and we sigh with relief. But we have not learnt its lesson. The only thing it tells us is that it is certain to come on again, if we do the same things. But the things are delightful to us. They are "worth the storm" we think; and we begin once more our pleasant sin. "Let the storm come," we cry; "we shall get through it again, if necessary." The end of that is not peace; no, nothing like peace. And the days will come on such a soul when it would give the world to have some quiet from sin and its fruits, and will not be able. Then the tempest will be too heavy for it; and it will go down in the night, silent and stubborn to the last.

There is another way in which men meet the tempests of life. It is the way of the fatalists, who may have faith in God, but not in a God who is the Father of men. If the storm come on them from without, having no apparent cause in their own act, "I have nothing," they say, "to do with this trouble. It is like a fever caught in a crowd. It is God's will; or, if there be no God, it is Nature's necessarian trick. And since I had nothing to do with it, I will do nothing to get out of it. If it clears, so much the better. If it does not, why, my shipwreck was written on my forehead."

So he speaks, but another may feel that the storm was, at least, apparently, of his own raising. "What the world calls my imprudence, or my temper, or the passionate desire which I would fulfil—these have brought this trouble on me; but the world is really wrong. I was made in this way by God, or heredity has made me so; these imprudences and tempers and desires were in me, and must have come out. No will of mine could have prevented them. My will to do them is as much fated as the rest. So the storm is fated also, and my rescue or not from it does not depend on me. My future was settled some millions of years ago. Wherefore, I have neither fear nor care; nor am I likely to ask for help. Why beseech the inexorable? Why weary myself with foolish prayer? I shall be sorry, I suppose, if I am overwhelmed, and glad if I find myself in the sunny islands again; but whether I am glad or sorry matters not a pin to imperturbable necessity; nay, my feelings are a part of that necessity. This is my faith, and in it I have peace. Calm reigns in my inner life, however loud the winds are without."

Peace! It is the peace of the desert where there is no life. Inactivity is not peace; and fatalism ends in the destruction of action. To put aside thought, as the fatalist does, is to lose the power of thinking; and to lose that power is not to be able to learn anything. And as to feel is only to torment oneself in vain, he loses also the power of feeling, or strives to lose it. Doing nothing, then; thinking, learning, and feeling nothing; that is his end, and no doubt there is calm in his soul. But he might as well be dead; and he is dead while he lives. It does not seem a very useful, noble, or beautiful way in which to meet the storms of life; nor does it enable us to do one atom of good to men. The way of faith in a Father is better—the way of Jesus —because it ennobles character, and enables us to strengthen men.

Again, there is a kind of faith, or of that which calls itself faith, which is of little good in the gale, and which leaves us as peaceless as before. An example of that is given to us in an addition made to this story of the calming of the sea, and which seems to have been made in order to fit the case of many during the persecutions. This is the story of Peter walking on the sea to meet Jesus. It is plainly symbolic. There were those who in the persecution put themselves into the way of martyrdom; wished to give a striking proof of their faith; affronted death on an impetuous impulse of excitement; and then, when torture and death were realised, broke down in fear and feebleness. Having no clear understanding of the dangers of temptation, their faith only an excited impulse, and not a rock-rooted conviction; they set forth triumphantly to walk on the tossing waves. "God will protect me," they cry; "I will take the plunge.

He will give His angels charge over me, lest I fall." This is to hunt for the storm, to believe in one's self more than in God, to seek to test our faith or to test God by running into spiritual danger which does not offer itself in the quiet way of duty.

Untried, then, ignorant, vain, having no calmness of faith, we enter into troubles which we have ourselves challenged, and all for a little time is well. But suddenly the wind grows louder, the waves heave and foam beneath our feet, our eyes are blinded by the gale, our ears deafened with its roar—all the rush and fierceness of the trial is upon us. In a moment fear has possession of us, and in the weakness born of fear we begin to sink. We realise that we have had only the semblance of faith; only transient excitement, not eternal trust; only weakness, not the strength of quiet faith.

And then we know that God

has been to us only an idol of sentiment to which our unreal emotions offered incense; and our faith only vanity. We understand then that human life is serious, that trouble and temptation are not to be played with, that God is a reality and our childhood to Him no dream. Then, if we have any earnestness in us at all, we learn what prayer actually is, know our weakness, get some sense of the realities of life, some conviction of God, and cry, "O my Father, save me lest I perish"; till at last we are stripped of all self-conceit, our self-will torn out of our hearts; and we are cast, stripped of unrealities, upon the shore of a new life, to begin again. It is a long time, after that experience, before we gain our peace.

The true faith is very different. It does not need to prove itself by challenging danger; but when the storm comes, it is ready to meet it, certain to overcome it;

because it knows that the storm is in the order of God, and that if we are true children, we shall be nearer, by fighting through it, to our Father. That is a steady, resolute, active quality—not the child of impulse, but the continuous movement of the whole nature in holy love towards union with God; not the ephemeral birth of sudden feeling that dies in fear or pain, but the long-growing, slowly-built conviction of the whole being —of intellect, conscience, imagination, affections, and spirit—each harmonised with the rest, each convinced, that the Almighty righteousness and love are ours, that God is ours, and that we are His.

In such a heart there is a great calm, the calm of activity which knows it is useful to mankind, for all its work is in God; the calm of perfect knowledge; the calm of absolute trust; the deeper calm of perfect love of Him whose very Being is the love of all. All storms may blow wildly round the ship of this faithful man, but he can afford to sleep if he be weary. And when others call on him for help, he comes to cheer, to comfort, to infuse his own faith into his fellow-men; and thus to still their storms. He has faith in himself because he has faith in God. And the result is courage, the mark and proof of perfect faith; courage to endure as well as to act; the power Jesus possessed, and by which He died; the power by which thousands have subdued the world, wrought righteousness, stopped the mouths of lions, out of weakness were made strong, and met in death the bridal hour of life—always tranquil and making tranquillity. Yes, we must have more than faith in ourselves; we must have faith in One beyond ourselves—to be entirely brave, to have peace in the midst of storms. He who can face death without an eyelid quivering cannot often face the hooting of the world. There are who have the courage to die, but not the courage to live. Saul was brave, but not brave enough to endure defeat or meet the wail of Israel.

But he who can cling to a righteous cause because he believes that God is in it, and that it is the right thing for man, at the very time when the world is pushing it over the precipice with contempt; he who can endure shame for the sake of righteousness, and bear the cruelty of lies for the sake of truth; who can be serene when all else despair, for he knows that God is Master of the world; who never lets go his grip, but tightens it closer round thoughts and aims that belong to truth, the more bitter and heavy grows the opposition of the world; and who can pass away, if need be, as Jesus passed, not by a glorious death in battle, but by the ignominy of the cross, alone, despised, apparently defeated, yet convinced of the future, and seeing the Father in the hour of his dissolution—he has the highest courage, the courage which makes him know that he is immortal; the courage which is absolute peace, the courage which is the serene and noble victory of faith, and which leaves to mankind the dearest legacy:—" Peace I leave with you—My peace I give unto you."

And now think again (that I may bind up the end of these sayings with the whole) of the little Church of Jesus when the waves of persecution beat upon it; think again of our own lives when in the fourth watch of the night the wind is contrary; think again of the great agonies of human kind heavily labouring in the tempest; and at last of Jesus, calm and content in conviction that His Father was always love and righteousness, bringing comfort and cheer to others—Himself at peace and giving peace.

And then you will understand, with self-reproach and yet inspiration to be like Him, all the meaning of His cry: "Why are ye fearful, O ye of little faith?"

God's Education of Man.

"Howbeit when He, the Spirit of Truth, is come, He will guide you into all truth."
JOHN XVI. 12.

WHEN Christ spoke these words the Apostles were clustered round Him after the Last Supper. It was a solemn hour. The past of His life lay now before His eyes. "It is finished," said His heart. The present was still full of work; for He had to fill the hearts of His followers with those conceptions which were to abide like seeds within their hearts until the time came to vivify them. But the present also held the future in it. In those few men, educated by Him; in their work, filled by God's Spirit; the redemption of the world was concentrated. It was as if He stood on a mountain-side, whence issued eleven streams, and saw each flowing through a different country, and changing the world, now a desert, into a garden of the Lord. He prophesied within Himself the future. He saw mankind redeemed. But none could share His onward glance, nor see what He saw in the past; none could understand. With the deepest desire to speak of all that lay in His soul, with that longing we have for utterance when the heart is full, He could not speak.

Why could He not speak? Not because the Apostles would not, but because they could not, comprehend. How could He tell them, so long as they were in their present state of mind, all He knew? They would only have said, "We cannot tell what He saith." So, at last, in His quiet way, He let His thoughts come to the surface for a moment: "I have got many things to say to you, but ye cannot bear them now.

When He, the Spirit of Truth, is come, He will guide you into all truth."

They had not grown enough in heart or soul to understand Him then. But then, swiftly, crowded into a few weeks, through the days of the Passion to the hour of Pentecost, enough of education came upon them to enable them to reach a higher level of spiritual life. And the education, as frequently happens in life, was given in a succession of tremendous emotions. Often, when we have been brought slowly to a certain point, that which is needed to make us turn into a new path comes upon us, shock after shock, in a month, a week, even a day. This is a common human experience, but not many have had it given to them in the quick and rushing, the uncommon, trials the Apostles suffered.

First came the betrayal, when shame dwelt upon their hearts, and the sense of utter failure darkened round their lives. Then came the death of Christ; and none can tell what a storm of emotion, trouble, confusion filled their hearts that night and day. Then came the sudden joy and wonder at the conviction that He was alive in another world. Joy was succeeded by unbelief, unbelief again followed by joy. Then came the five weeks in Galilee. Back at their work, musing on what had happened, their souls slowly opened in meditation as they fished by the lake, or walked at evening by the shore, where they had so often been with Him. Then came the sense that if they were to realise Him it must now be no longer as a living man, but as an inward spirit. Then came the days of waiting at Jerusalem; the pause that fell upon their lives before the great change of Pentecost. They were alone, a few men and women and children who had clung to Him through life, and still clung to His memory. Alternate hope and fear, though hope predominated, filled their hearts; and in them and around them, as they prayed, all the past life of Christ grew into harmony and unity in their souls. Thoughts knit themselves to thoughts, feelings joined themselves to feelings, till at last they were fully prepared to enter upon a new life.

Into a few weeks all that experience was concentrated. The men who had gone through it did not come out at the other side of it the same men. Every point on which I have touched made a new world of feeling and thought in their hearts. They were a century older in intellect, in knowledge, in emotion, in love, in power, and in capacity both to do and to receive. And now that they were so changed—now was the time when many of the things Christ could not say to them at the Last Supper could be said; when they could be guided into further truth. They could bear it now, and then—the day of Pentecost arrived. They were filled with the Spirit. They knew what their Master meant when He said: "I will see you again, and your heart shall rejoice, and your joy no man taketh from you. When He, the Spirit of Truth, is come, He will guide you into all truth."

From all this, one principle arises. Revelation is measured out to mankind in nations, in societies, and in individuals, by the capacity to receive it, and God educates us through the circumstances of life up to that capacity. It is the law in accord with which God educates you and me, and every individual soul; and it is the law by which He educates also the vast personality of the human race. As the capacity of seeing light and truth increases, and as the power of feeling and knowing grows in mankind, so grows the light; so works the Spirit of God, year by year, age by age, never ceasing, never less living than in earlier times.

But we may bring this matter very close to ourselves. We have lived with God in our childhood and youth, all unconscious, perhaps, but still so near to Him that we never asked ourselves whether He was with us or not. We were educated by Him without knowing it; and when we stepped into manhood, in the inspiration with which we began our work, and, in the hope with which we looked forward, we heard like a prophecy these words, "I will guide you into truth."

Then came the world upon us. How busy we were; all the day long at work; and as our special work defined itself, and we were full of hope and strength, with what eagerness we pursued our aims, with what hope we rose in the morning, how full the day, how well earned the rest at night. Absorbed in the present, how could we think of that dim future, far away, of that unseen God who claimed our thoughts? And God, looking at us then, and loving us, said: "I have many things to say to you, but ye cannot bear them now; My voice will not be heard, nor, if I spoke, is your heart yet educated to desire or receive My truth." At last, in the very midst of all our restless activity—it may be when a little weariness comes of long-continued labour—we pause for a week, or a month, and in some hush of the life of the world, we hear the voice of God: "I will guide you into all truth." And we do not understand Him. "What does it mean? Why this strange voice, as of something beyond my daily life? Truth! Why, the only truth I want is that which lies before me here in this world."

Many a time that experience comes; and again and again in the turmoil of the world and the noise of work the voice of God is drowned.

At last, suddenly, the sky darkens. A rush of events, such as came to the Apostles, comes upon us. Shock after shock invades our life; betrayal of love, or betrayal of friendship, the shattering of business, or the death of one who was the staff of life; sickness, or pain, or bitter agony of heart. We are silent, but the mainspring of existence is broken, and we know it. Life, for years, perhaps, is very hard to live. At last, by the very hardness of life, by the very pain which has finally driven us from our last refuge in this world, we begin to meditate on God. Thoughts spring up which say, "*Whose* is this work? It is not mine." And then, like the Apostles while they waited at Jerusalem, we think back over our life. We study, in the sorrow of imagination, God's hand in it, and in the new, strange light of all we have gone through, we seem to see God, to hear Him, to believe. It is as if we listened to Him saying, "Dost thou *now* understand? The time is coming fast when I will guide thee into truth."

Then, like the Apostles, also we wait in obedience. For often it is all we can then do. There is nothing but a dim hope, and we can only go on bearing inwardly, day by day, our pain, with enough fortitude to say nothing. Only now we have enough courage also to obey God's will, so far as we know it. We strive to love others, to do good to them; we undertake the duties of life cheerfully, and love them because the loving of them brings us nearer to God—till at last we begin to feel that all sorrow is nothing, and all pain worthy of forgetting; if we can feel God at last to be truly ours, and know that though our earthly life decay His presence is enough to make all things new.

And then, finally, arises the last attitude of the Apostles—prayer. "Out of the depths I cry unto Thee, O God. Answer me, my Father! I want nothing now, but the consciousness of Thy presence; to know that Thou art mine, and I Thy child for ever. My soul is athirst for Thee and Thee alone."

That is education. At last we can bear the new light, the new life. And it comes now that we are capable of receiving it. Suddenly, the house of life is shaken, there is a sound from heaven in the chambers of the heart; all the windows fly open, and the light of God's morning streams in upon the soul; a rushing, mighty wind freshens the woods of feeling and animates the new blossoms of thought. It fills the whole estate of life. Our Pentecost has come.

But it is not the final Pentecost. We have not learnt all yet. No sooner is the first joy of revelation over, no sooner is the new life begun on these new impulses, than we hear again God's voice, "I will guide you into all truth. I have yet many things to show to you." Year by year, as the power of receiving grows, new truth is communicated. It is an endless growth, and it will never cease.

All growth is joy, the consciousness of it our very greatest joy. But until growth becomes the easy habit of the soul, it is dashed with sorrow and pain. Only when we reach the summit of endeavour is our joy complete. But the time will arrive when the growth will be difficult enough for effort but not for exhaustion; when every step will be delight; when in a newer and more inspiring world God will be closer to us, and life be always enkindled, always ready, always at full sail before a flowing, uplifting wind. That will be perfect joy. Many things that God could not say to us on earth He will say then: it will be a new Pentecost. A rushing, mighty wind, indeed, shall fill our being; new tongues, tongues of fire, will be ours with which we shall declare new thoughts, and speak new things. The Spirit will give us utterance.

But, even then, in the very heart of that divine revelation, we shall know that God's education of us will not be final. For God is infinite, and eternity cannot exhaust the education He gives to us. As each period of growth reaches its end in the heavenly world, we shall again hear with joy the ancient words of progress: "I have yet many things to say to you, but ye cannot bear them now."

Faithfulness until Death.

"Be thou faithful until death, and I will give thee a crown of life."—Rev. ii. 10.

The words themselves are inspiration; they sound like a trumpet in the midst of the battle; and I would that the passing emotion they awake might be so continuous, as not to be able to refrain from expression in the thought and action of a life. The emotion which flies through the soul, like a sparrow through the Northumbrians' hall, is pleasant, but having no result in act is worthless. Only that emotion is worthy which completes itself in form. Moreover, the habit of emotions which pass away, and the cherishing of them for the sake of the flitting succession of pleasures that they give, creates a positive evil in the character. It makes the character faithless. The new emotion blows out the candle of the old, and its successor extinguishes it in turn. Nothing is kept, and nothing is truly loved. The new alone is sought for, and to seek only the new is not to be able to be faithful.

Yet we are the children of emotion. It is, in our lives, first in the field—before intelligence, before conscience, even before will. Therefore, considering the swiftness with which emotion tends to change, the first thing we have to do when the will has awakened, and conscience and intelligence are born; and the first thing children should be taught to do, is to learn how to hold fast our emotions, when they are noble, and to put them into shape. When children are allowed to avoid that effort, and to take pleasure in the mere drift of feelings through them, they are being brought up to become faithless characters. When they are trained in the other way, they have made the first step towards faithfulness, as well as towards the continuity of aspiration. They become men to whom the text means something more than the kindling of the senses as at the sound of a trumpet. It means the unfaltering effort of a life, its nobility and its spiritual joy.

But it meant more to the early Christian people. To us, the words are partly metaphorical; but they had no metaphorical meaning when they were written. The persecution of Nero had told the Christians what they might expect. Death was the least pain which the world against them had in its quiver. They were hunted like the wild beast of the woods. They were tortured, exposed to the hatred of the crowd who cheered the lion and the wild bull who tore and dragged them to death. Through these physical woes, as well as through the spiritual struggles that we have, they had to persevere, were they to be faithful. Those who kept the faith were obliged to look agony of body and death in the face.

Men who began the Christian race had then to count the cost, and resolve to pay it. They had to give up *all*, or at least be ready at a moment to give up all—home, friends, wealth, worldly honour— and to take Christ instead, and death. The rich, of whom there were many, had harder temptations to face than the poor. Not only did all the good things of the world which they were bound to surrender appeal to them, but every inducement was held out to them— of love, and property, and fame—to lead them to sacrifice to the Emperor. On their ears, even louder than on the ears of the poor, fell this trumpet-call, "Be thou faithful unto death," and to their eternal honour the greater number of them obeyed the call, and paid the glorious penalty.

Faithful to what? To a selfish aim, to a political or religious party cry, to a cause which offered to them material rewards? No; but faithful unto death to the great ideas of Christ; to the conception of God's fatherhood; of man's brotherhood; of communion which could not be broken, with the Divine and with the human; faithful to the conception of the Church universal, and the immortality of all its members; faithful in life to the character of the Father—to goodness, to truth, to justice, to purity within and without; to an ideal perfection which was certain at last to be attained; faithful to their Master, Christ, who had established in them these truths; faithful to Him with so passionate a love that it were easier to die in torment than to betray His name or swerve from His example; faithful to His work, which was love of men to the death, pardon for the sinner, forgiveness of enemies, absolute sacrifice of life for love, death that wrong might die, death for the cause of man. These were the matters to which they were faithful, and not one of them brought with it a worldly reward. There was not one which was not spiritual, which did not proclaim that the spiritual world—that is, the world of love and faith and righteousness—was the only world for men, and that, in comparison with it, the material world and all its rewards were nothing at all.

And what was their reward? It also was spiritual. It was the consciousness of union with God, and through Him, because He was *our* Father, union with all humanity. It was to feel themselves citizens of an eternal kingdom which annihilated all the differences, castes and classes of earth, but annihilated them that it might make one nation out of all nations, and all men brothers in that universal nationality. It was to feel themselves at one with all the noble dead who now dwelt in the City of God. It was that they had in all their sorrows, the immortal sympathy of God and Jesus, of angels and just men made perfect. They were never alone, none were ever lost to them. The whole universe of spirit was their friend. It was that the crown of eternal life was theirs; not a life in after days so coarsely imagined —a life of rewards such as those given on earth—but the continuance of the eternal life they already had on earth; the Divine life of the soul; in which righteousness should become perfect, which should be immortal union with Justice, Purity, and Truth—the life of God Himself: that life of absolute love which some are fools enough to say is a selfish thing to desire; but which is, on the contrary, the transformation of every touch of selfishness into love; love so full, so absolute, and so undying, that never for one moment, through all eternity, shall we think of ourselves again. Absence of self-desire—there are religions which think to gain that in ceasing to be—in the destruction of personal life. But our religion's highest honour is that through it we gain absence of self-desire through fulness of life; that personality remains, and is at its height in absolute loss of self. These blessings were their reward, and to desire them, to live for them, enforces and secures unselfishness. It is the greatest glory of the human race to live for them, and die for them. It is to live and die, as Jesus did, for love, since to love like God is to possess them all. Immortal Life is equal to Immortal Love.

This was the meaning of the text to the early Christians. It should be its meaning for us. The conditions of life, indeed, are changed, but the things for which we should live and die faithfully are the same; and the fruit of them is the same now as then.

But the change of conditions, while it has made the physical trials less, has doubled the spiritual difficulties. We are not persecuted as Nero persecuted the Christians, but we have twice as many temptations in life. We must not regret our greater knowledge, our more complex life, our own time. Out of such regret nothing comes but base retirement from the strife. But we are all the more bound to be faithful unto death to the spiritual, since we are so overwhelmed with the material. Alas! it is this faithfulness to the spiritual that Society has largely abandoned. Luxury, comfort, ease, wealth, the tyranny of knowledge, the belief only in the palpable and the probable, the competition for money, the doing of art for money—these have driven life down into the mud, and our society is not far from that degree of baseness which, when it is reached, dooms the society. All that men say now of the splendour and wealth of England, and all the boasting of the upper classes in this country, while deep below lies a morass of misery and ignorance and crime and despairing poverty, in which monsters of the slime are moving and devouring, is dreadful to hear. It is glorying in degradation. Their luxury is filth, and their wealth is villainy. All luxury and comfort, gained for selfish ends alone, is corrupt; and the tendency to consider them to be the whole of life belongs to every class, to the poor as well as to the rich. Have they been gained, and are they established, by love of man ? Has the faith in the universal Fatherhood of God anything to do with them, or have they been gained by trampling that faith into the dust? What would Christ and His doctrine of the brotherhood of all, of giving up our lives to men, say to the fortunes which are made out of the misery of the poor, and which are spent to the detriment and ruin of the real capital of the country, of the men, women, and children who are the vitals of England? Can we say for one moment that a great part of our society has any faith in Jesus, or that He is to it more than a plague and a weariness? You read in every daily paper what we are doing, what the life is which many in this country are leading. Is that life faithful unto death for the spiritual—for love and truth and justice? No; and its doom, unless it repent, will be the crown of death.

But there are others who do not live in this idling, gambling, corrupt, greedy fashion; but who have no more faith than they in the spiritual life, that is, in a life which is directed by ideas which are above the material world, belief in a Father in whom the race of man is contained, and by the duties towards men which follow on that belief; men who have no hope for man, and no happier hopes for the race. These are weary of the whole matter, and retire from the strife, some in sorrow, some in cynicism. They have had their dreams; they have done some work; but they have found out that their dreams had no basis, and that their work was no use. Henceforth they will sing their songs alone. It is not very noble, but it is very comfortable. They have built a wall round the park of their life to shut out the world. The rooms in their house are filled with knowledge and with art and song. Not a cry from the suffering world penetrates into this refuge of peace; nothing to disturb the pleasant solitude in which the history of man is like a picture on the wall, and his agony of battle is seen, as one sees a tragedy from a stall in a theatre.

It is agreeable, artistic, poetic, though the true artist and the true poet are not there. They are in the battle; if they be true artist, true poet, they know the sorrow and joy, the torment and the strife of man, if they write well and paint well. Let the word pass then—we are not likely to confuse these persons with the true artist. But wherever they may be, this life of theirs is *not* being faithful unto death, but faithful unto self; and the crown it wins is not the crown of life, but the crown of death—death of high imagination, death of true emotion, death of eager thought, death of those passions which bear us beyond ourselves, death in us of man, and therefore death of God. They think they have these things—their life, imagination, passion, and the rest —and for a time they may have their remnants. But they have divided themselves from the common heart of man, and these great qualities, fed no more from that rockborn and perennial fountain, droop and die. Then they make false images of them and worship them from degradation to degradation.

This is one of the curses of an over-rich, an over-easy society— vast numbers of comfortable middle-class people, who do plenty of work for themselves, but little for mankind; who nurse their dainty sympathies; and who, refusing every idea that troubles their ease, despising every emotion which in their youth led them to join in the great strife and labour of the world towards good, are sodden in selfishness, till humanity becomes a vision of the night, and God a phantom of the brain.

This is the result of not having clear, passionately felt principles, of having no convictions of truths for which we would sacrifice our life. The natural sloth of the mind then passes into indifference to everything except ourselves. Nothing outside matters much, we then think, except our own interest and our own fancies.

It was different in that Apostolic time. Men had then clear convictions, and they were faithful to them. They believed that what they held as main principles were necessary for the welfare of the human race, and they would rather have died than have swerved from them for a moment. That earnestness, that conviction of necessary truth, is what so many of us need in a world where beliefs tend to become indefinite and indifferent. "It does not matter much," they say, "under what form we worship God, what principles we hold, what truths we accept. God is seen in many ways; He fulfils Himself in various fashions." Faiths have many sides; principles vary in form. That is true; but it argues looseness of mind and weakness of will not to be able to choose one way—one set of principles for life—and when we have chosen them, to cling to them. If we change our convictions—as we sometimes must, under the pressure of God, in order to be true to conscience—we ought to change with the whole mass of our nature and character going with the change. The drifting habit so many have—the indifferent swinging to and fro from one set of religious, political, and moral ideas to another, and then to another—is not a thing to boast of, but is rooted in unfaithfulness of character, in inconstancy of mind. If, having any faith at all, we have no clear conceptions of what it is most useful to the human race to have taught everywhere, and best for us ourselves to live out plainly before the world, we have no faith worth having; and we shall not realise God, or moral or social truth with any reality, nor impress ourselves with any force upon the world. It is our business to get what we think and believe into lucid form, and then to support it with all our power, influence, and presence. Faithfulness is claimed from us by God and man.

It is not faithfulness to our conceptions to be lured away from the action due to them or their support by any pleasure or any fancy, or by the desires of ambition, of society, or the world. It is not faithfulness to be ashamed of their reproach, if they have any reproach in the eyes of men. It is not faithfulness to be indifferent to their advance, or to fail to support them by our presence in public; to be half in them and half outside of them in other ideas.

It is not faithfulness, by any act of ours, to let lookers-on think that our belief lies loose on us like a garment which we wear or not at pleasure.

No; whatever you profess, cling to with all your soul. Whatever ship you sail in, fly your flag; and let all the world know clearly under which banner you sail the seas. There is no indifference, no to and fro, where there is faithfulness. As a man clings to his wife, so should he cling to the truths, forms, and faith which he has chosen. Let him marry what form he likes, but having married, let him be faithful all round to his faith. That constancy, that faithfulness, is what moves the world. By that, the ideas we think worthy and precious are spread far and wide for the use and good of men. By that, religious, political, social, moral, artistic, educational, societies win their way, and there is no other way the wit of men can compass. By that, also, we ourselves attain slowly the most noble of all the virtues for the practical strength of character in man or woman—the virtue of enduring faithfulness. I recommend these considerations at a time when indifferentism is exalted almost into a virtue. Have convictions and cling to them. Gain principles of faith, of morals, of human action; love them earnestly, and shape them into undeviating action.

Once more, there is another tendency in modern Society to which the text speaks home. Indifference sinks into a belief that this world is too bad to be cured, too vile to live in. I have often said that this belief is the child of a too comfortable, too science-ridden, too luxurious a Society. The miserable, the oppressed, the starving sometimes preach this doctrine when the contrasts of life are too horrible to them. But few among them keep it. Misery, poverty, desperate battle, rage of indignation, unspeakable suffering —this is not the soil in which hatred and scorn of life flourish, but rather that in which optimism roots itself most deeply. It is among these that almost all of the Utopias of the earth have been formed and preached. It is, on the contrary, among the comfortable philosophers, among those who have time to despise humanity —or to pity it, from a distance— among those who are wearied with luxury, and bored with the dregs of all enjoyment, that this degrading belief grows up and flourishes. It is the product of an enervated, idle, and decaying society. Its saddest symptom is that those who hold it boast themselves in it, are even excited in its propaganda. The excitement is, in itself, not a bad thing. One sees in it a certain vigour of which God will make use hereafter when they know better. But it is a bad thing to be excited about base prophecies. To prove that to be nothing is better than to be alive; that life itself is only a battle against misery on one side, and *ennui* on the other; that egoism is the only motive of man; that love is only the blind desire of sense or of reproduction; that death is the only blessing, for it destroys us; that all the work of humanity is a motiveless battle — *that* is not worth the proving. It is to try and prove what is base, and out of it comes no nobility. To believe it would degrade the race, and turn the good into the wicked, and the wicked into devils. It is a doctrine which is faithful unto death in another way than the writer of our text meant, and its crown is the crown of corruption.

I thank God that there are thousands in this country who have not bowed the knee to these Baals, who have neither given themselves over to the world, nor retired from the work of humanity, nor declared that everything is base, and death its only remedy; and who have resolved, in humility and in failure, in sorrow or in joy, to be faithful to God and man unto death, whether there be a crown of life or not. There is this crown, and it comes none the less to those who do not believe in it; if they are faithful to the life and spirit of Jesus, who lived and died for love of man—the child of God. These are men and women whom we honour, with whom we desire to work, whose aims are the same as ours, though we wish they built their labour on our foundation. They believe in man, hope for him and love him, and so far, they and we are one in the work of Jesus Christ. They do not share His faith or ours in a Brotherhood held in God the Father; but in the end the loving work will create the faith. I wish we could work more heartily together. It would be a miserable matter if, for the sake of religious opinions, we were to split into two unconnected efforts the opposition we both make to the luxury, materialism, indifference, and despair of progress, which are the true enemies of the human race.

Let us not only be faithful to the death, but faithful to one another. Schism in the ranks of those at war against selfishness, in men or national life, is the worst of pities. It strikes at the root of progress, for it strikes at the love of one another. Therefore let us join our armies for a great purpose, for the bettering of mankind by love; bring our thoughts, our ideals, our action into one movement of sacrifice for this purpose. Let us cease to attack, and only support, one another; and whether we confess God or not, He will be with us; whether we own Christ or not as our Master, we shall be doing His work.

There is an uphill strife before us. It is the old strife against the lust of the flesh, the lust of wealth, the desire to get everything for oneself out of our fellow men, the desperate greed of self-interest, within ourselves and without us in the world. In conquering these evil things is the true honour and salvation of our country. In the fate of the battle all over the world the fate of humanity is contained. Be faithful to your cause, faithful to death, and we shall have the crown of life; for the more we labour, sacrifice, and die in this strife, the more we shall love, and love is the Crown of Life.

LONDON:
W. SPEAIGHT AND SONS, PRINTERS,
FETTER LANE, E.C.

www.ingramcontent.com/pod-product-compliance
Lightning Source LLC
Chambersburg PA
CBHW022140160426
43197CB00009B/1362